Twenty to Ma...

Knitted Cakes

Susan Penny

Search Press

First published in Great Britain 2008

Search Press Limited
Wellwood, North Farm Road,
Tunbridge Wells, Kent TN2 3DR

Reprinted 2009 (twice), 2010

Text copyright © Susan Penny 2008

Photographs by Roddy Paine Photographic Studio

Photographs and design copyright
© Search Press Ltd 2008

ISBN: 978-1-84448-361-7

Suppliers
If you have difficulty in obtaining any of the
materials and equipment mentioned in this book,
then please visit the Search Press website for
details of suppliers: www.searchpress.com

Printed in Malaysia.

Abbreviations

beg: beginning

dec: decrease (by working two
stitches together)

g st: garter stitch (knit every row)

inc: increase (by working into the front and
back of the stitch)

K: knit

K2tog: knit two stitches together

P: purl

P2tog: purl two stitches together

rib: ribbing (one stitch knit, one stitch purl)

st(s): stitch(es)

st st: stocking stitch (one row knit, one
row purl)

Contents

Introduction

Knitting is a craft that has simmered away on my creative back burner for years, without me ever having the time or the opportunity to turn up the heat – that is until now. After all the sewing, embroidery, cross stitch and crafts books I have worked on, this is my first book on knitting – and what fun it has been! I have discovered, to my delight, the modern wool shop. Gone are the days when the assistant can offer you double knitting in battleship grey or donkey brown. The dark, dusty shelves stacked with utilitarian wool have been replaced by a sea of colours and textures. Row upon row of gorgeous wool – soft, sensuous mohair next to natural organic cotton, and fun, funky polyester next to soft merino.

As you can see from the projects in this book I have tried out many of these wonderful yarns. The projects are aimed at all ages and abilities – my kids love the modern look of the Crazy Cup Cakes, and have picked up their needles to have a go. So whatever you choose to knit, have fun!

Susan A Penny

Chocolate Gateau

Materials:

2 balls double knitting – 1 chocolate and
 1 cream

1 ball fluffy polyester yarn – cream

18 small, brown wooden beads

Cardboard for insert, 9 x 37cm (3½ x 14½in)

Toy stuffing

Needles:

1 pair 3.25mm (UK 10; US 3) knitting needles

Instructions:

Back and top of gateau

Cast on 14 sts in chocolate.
Rows 1–10: st st, starting with a K row.
Rows 11–14: change to fluffy yarn. Continue in st st.
Rows 15–24: change back to chocolate and continue in st st.
Row 25: purl across a knit row.
Rows 26–30: ** starting with a P row, work in st st.
Row 31: K1, K2tog, K to last 3 sts, K2tog, K1.
Rows 32–34: starting with a P row, work in st st.
Row 35: K1, K2tog to last 3 sts, K2tog, K1.
Rows 36–38: starting with a P row, work in st st.

Row 39: K1, K2tog, knit to last 3 sts, K2tog, K1.
Rows 40–42: starting with a P row, work in st st.
Row 43: K1, K2tog, K2, K2tog, K1.
Rows 44–46: starting with a P row, work in st st.
Row 47: K1, K2tog, K2tog, K1.
Row 48: purl.
Row 49: K2tog, K2tog.
Row 50: purl.
Row 51: K2tog. Break yarn and pull thread through last stitch. **

Base of gateau

Pick up and knit 14 sts across the cast-on row of the gateau back. Starting with a purl row work exactly as the top of the gateau from ** to **.

Sides of gateau

The sides of the gateau are knitted in one piece.

Cast on 48 sts in chocolate.
Rows 1–10: st st.
Rows 11–14: change to fluffy yarn. Continue in st st.
Rows 15–24: change back to chocolate and continue in st st.
Cast off.

Piped cream

Make two lengths of 3 chocolate cream swirls; two lengths with 3 light-coloured cream swirls; one length with 2 light-coloured cream swirls; and a single light-coloured cream swirl.

Cast on 1 st in chocolate or cream.
Row 1: ** K1, P1, K1, P1, K1 into the cast-on stitch [5 sts].
Row 2: slip 1, K3, leave the last st unworked. Work on the 3 centre sts until row 6.
Row 3: P3, leave last st.
Row 4: K3, leave last st.
Row 5: P3, leave last st.
Row 6: K4.
Row 7: P1, P2tog, P2tog.
Row 8: K2tog, K1.
Row 9: P2tog. ** [1 st].
Break yarn and pull through the remaining stitch – this will make a single cream swirl. To make a length of piped cream, repeat rows 1–9 from ** to **.

Making up

Attach one short edge of the gateau side to the back edge of the cake, making sure that the strips of cream-coloured gateau filling line up correctly. Repeat for the other side. Sew on the gateau base. Fold the strip of cardboard into a triangular shape and fit it inside the gateau to line the sides and back of the cake. It is important to make the cardboard shape slightly larger than the knitting, so that the knitting is stretched as it is sewn in place. This will make a neater finish. Stuff the cake with toy stuffing and sew on the top. Sew the two lengths of chocolate cream swirls to the back of the gateau – one along the bottom edge and one along the top edge. Attach the light-coloured cream swirls to the top of the gateau, then sew on the wooden beads.

Iced Doughnut

Materials:

2 balls 4 ply – 1 beige and 1 pink

Pink seed beads

Pink bugle beads

Toy stuffing

Needles:

Set of 4 x 3.25mm (UK 10; US 3) knitting
needles with points at both ends

Instructions:

Cast on 30 sts using beige wool – 10 sts on
each of 3 needles.

Rounds 1–6: knit.

Round 7: knit, increasing 2 sts randomly on
each needle [12 sts on each needle; 36 sts
in total].

Rounds 8–10: continue, increasing 2 sts
randomly on each needle until there are 18 sts
on each [54 sts in total].

Rounds 11–18: knit.

Rounds 19–26: break yarn and change to pink.
Knit 8 rounds.

Rounds 27–30: dec 2 sts randomly on each
needle until 10 sts on each needle [30 sts
in total].

Rounds 31–36: knit.

Cast off.

Making up

Stretch the stitching round into a doughnut
shape and fill with toy stuffing. Using matching
wool sew the doughnut together. Decorate
with seed and bugle beads.

*The white-iced doughnut is knitted using cream
and beige 4 ply wool and decorated with seed and
bugle beads in pastel shades.*

Coffee Cup Cake

Materials:

2 balls pure merino – 1 cream and 1 coffee

1 ball 100% cotton 4 ply – white

Pearl bead

60mm (2¼in) polystyrene craft ball

Toy stuffing

Needles:

1 pair 4mm (UK 8; US 6) knitting needles

1 pair 2.25mm (UK 13; US 1) knitting needles

1 pair 3.25mm (UK 10; US 3) knitting needles

Instructions:

Top of cake

Cast on 40 sts in cream wool using
4mm needles.

Rows 1–4: st st for 4 rows.

Rows 5–10: change to coffee and g st for
6 rows.

Row 11: (K4, K2tog) to last 4 sts, K4 [34 sts].

Row 12: knit.

Row 13: knit, decreasing 6 sts randomly across
row [28 sts].

Row 14: knit.

Row 15: knit, decreasing 4 sts randomly across
row [24 sts].

Row 16: knit.

Break yarn, leaving a long end. Thread through
stitches on needle and draw up tightly.

Side of case

Cast on 60 sts using white cotton 4 ply and
2.25mm needles.

Rows 1–11: K1, P1 across row for 11 rows.

Row 12: inc every second P st across row.

Cast off.

Base of case

Cast on 10 sts using white cotton 4 ply and
2.25mm needles. Work in st st.

Row 1: * purl.

Row 2: knit, increasing 1 st at beg and end
of row. *

Rows 3–8: repeat rows 1 and 2 from * to *
[18 sts].

Rows 9–11: continue in st st.

Rows 12–18: dec 1 st at beg and end of every K
row [10 sts].

Row 19: purl.

Cast off.

Flower

Using 3.25mm needles and cream follow the
instruction for a single swirl of piped cream on
page 6. Break yarn and thread it through the
single stitch on the needle. Repeat for
each petal.

Making up

Join the side seam of the cup cake case, then
stitch the bottom in place. Join the side seam
of the cup cake top. Pull up the thread holding
the stitches at the top of the cake, and darn the
thread end in to hold it firmly in place. Attach
the petals to the top of the cake, adding a
bead to the centre. Using cream wool, make
French knots on the top of the cake. Position
the cake top inside the cup cake case. Insert a
polystyrene craft ball, adding some stuffing to
pad out the shape, then catch stitch the top to
the bottom.

*The mocha cup cake is stitched in
chocolate-coloured wool and decorated
with dark wooden beads.*

Birthday Cake

Materials:

2 balls double knitting – 1 pink and 1 cream

Small amount pure merino – cream

Small amount double knitting – dark pink

2 red bugle beads

4 pink seed beads

12mm (½in) pink ribbon, 80cm (31½in)

Cardboard for insert, 10 x 51cm (4 x 20in)

Drinking straw

Needles:

1 pair 3.25mm (UK 10; US 3) knitting needles

Instructions:

Top and base of cake

For cake top, cast on 25 sts in pink.

Rows 1–25: st st.

Cast off. Repeat for the base.

Sides of cake

The sides of the cake are knitted in one piece.

Cast on 78 sts in pink.

Rows 1–28: st st.

Cast off.

Flower

Cast on 28 sts in pink.

Row 1: (K1, cast off 5 sts) to end [8 sts].

Break yarn and use a needle to pull it through the remaining 8 sts – this will make four petals. Secure the wool end with a few stitches to hold the petals together.

Candle

Cast on 17 sts using cream pure merino.

Rows 1–5: st st.

Cast off.

Flame

Cast on 2 sts in dark pink.

Row 1: knit.

Row 2: inc every st [4 sts].

Rows 3–4: knit.

Row 5: repeat row 2 [6 sts].

Rows 6–7: knit.

Row 8: K2tog, K2, K2tog [4 sts].

Rows 9–10: knit.

Row 11: K2tog, K2tog [2 sts].

Row 12: K2tog.

Piped cream

Make two lengths of piped cream in cream double knitting, each with 16 cream swirls, following the instructions on page 6.

Making up

From the cardboard make a box 10cm (4in) long x 7.5cm (3in) wide x 9.5cm (3¾in) deep. Make a small hole in the centre top for the candle. Wrap the knitted side panel around the box with the seam at the centre back. Sew the edges together with matching wool. Place the top and base of the cake in place and stitch to the edges of the side panel. Stitch the piped cream swirls around the top and bottom edges of the cake. Using cream wool, make French knots in a pattern on the sides and top of the cake. Stitch the pink flower to the to p of the cake, directly over the hole in the cardboard. For the candle, wrap the rectangle of knitting around the drinking straw and stitch it in place – the straw should be left longer than the stitching so that it can be pushed down into the box. Push the drinking straw into the hole in the box through the knitting. Secure with a few neat stitches. Stitch seed beads to each flower petal. Attach the flame to the candle, adding a bugle bead to each side. Tie the pink ribbon around the cake.

Fruit Tart

Materials:

1 ball 4 ply – beige

1 ball fluffy mohair acrylic mix – cream

Small amounts of 4 ply in pink, orange and yellow

Small amounts of double knitting in red and mauve

Small amounts of cotton yarn in lime green

Black, red and pink seed beads

Jar lid for pastry case insert, approximately 8cm (3¼in) diameter

Toy stuffing

Needles:

1 pair 3.25mm (UK 10; US 3) knitting needles

Set of 4 x 2.25mm (UK 13; US 1) knitting needles with points at both ends

Instructions:

Tart case

Using 4 ply beige, cast on 96 sts with double-ended needles – 32 sts on each of 3 needles.
Rounds 1–11: (K2, P2) for 11 rounds.
Round 12: purl.
Round 13: knit, decreasing 2 sts randomly on each needle.
Continue decreasing on each round until 1 st remains on each needle. Break yarn and pull through the remaining 3 sts.

Cream for inside tart

Using 3.25mm needles and cream, cast on 10 sts.
Rows 1–2: st st, starting with a K row.
Row 3: (K1, inc 1 st) 5 times across row [15 sts].
Row 4: purl.
Row 5: (K1, inc 1 st) to end [22 sts].
Row 6: purl.
Row 7: (K1, inc 1 st) to end [33 sts].
Row 8: purl.
Row 9: (K1, inc 1 st) to end [49 sts].
Rows 10–24: continue in st st.
Row 25: (K2tog, K1) to end [33 sts].
Row 26: purl.
Row 27: (K2tog, K1) to end [22 sts].
Row 28: purl.
Row 29: (K2tog, K1) to end [15 sts].
Row 30: purl.
Row 31: (K2tog, K1) to end [10 sts].
Row 32: purl.
Cast off.

Orange and lemon slices and raspberries

Make one orange slice, one lemon slice and three raspberries.

Using 3.25mm needles and appropriate colour, cast on 2 sts. Work in st st, starting with a K row.
Row 1: ** * inc every st to end [4 sts].
Row 2: purl.
Row 3: inc every st to end [8 sts].
Row 4: purl. *
Row 5: inc every st to end [16 sts].
Row 6: purl. **
Cast off.

Berries and kiwi slices

Make eleven berries and two kiwi slices.

Using 3.25mm needles and mauve or lime green, cast on 2 sts and work as given for slices and raspberries from * to *.
Row 5: K2tog to end [4sts].
Row 6: purl.
Row 7: K2tog to end [2sts].
Row 8: P2tog.
Break yarn and thread it through the last stitch.

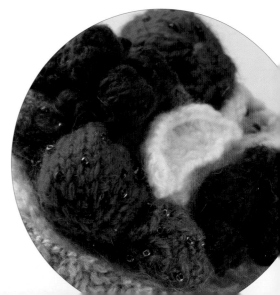

Strawberries

Make two strawberries.

Cast on 2 sts using 3.25mm needles and red wool. Work 2 rows in st st.
Work as for slices and raspberries from ** to **.
Next row: inc every st to end [32 sts].
Starting with a P row, work in st st for 7 rows.
Cast off.

Making up

To finish each kiwi slice, stitch black seed beads in a circle on both sides. Sew up the side seam of each raspberry with right sides together – you will have a funnel shape. Turn right-side out. Insert a small ball of toy stuffing, pushing it well down into the raspberry. Use the same coloured wool to make a few criss-cross stitches just inside the raspberry – this will close in the stuffing and gather the top slightly. Decorate with pink seed beads. Sew up the side seam of each strawberry in the same way. Stuff completely, then gather the top and secure with a few stitches. Decorate with red seed beads. To finish a berry, gather up the knitted circle and secure the thread. Stitch five or six berries together to make a bunch. Secure the long thread in the middle of the tart case with a few stitches. Stretch the tart case over the jar lid. Lay a small amount of toy stuffing in the case then spread the knitted cream over the top, securing it at the edges with a few stitches. Arrange the fruit and secure through the cream with a few neat stitches.

Jazzy Cake

Materials:

1 ball pure merino wool – off-white

1 ball double knitting – multi-coloured

Small amount of decorative, multi-coloured yarn

Small amount of fluffy polyester yarn – cream

Multi-coloured seed beads

Multi-coloured bugle beads

10mm (½in) multi-coloured ribbon, 36cm (14¼in)

Toy stuffing

Needles:

1 pair 3.25mm (UK 10; US 3) knitting needles

Instructions:

Iced top

Cast on 10 sts in off-white using 3.25mm needles.

Rows 1–15: work in st st, starting with a K row, increasing 1 st at beg and end of each K row [26 sts].

Row 16: purl.

Row 17: knit.

Row 18: purl.

Rows 19–33: continue in st st, decreasing 1 st at beg and end of each K row [10 sts].

Row 34: purl.

Cast off.

Side of cake

Using multi-coloured double knitting and 3.25mm needles, cast on 17 sts.

Rows 1–90: st st.

Cast off.

Base of cake

Using multi-coloured double knitting and 3.25mm needles, cast on 8 sts.

Rows 1–2: work in st st, starting with a K row.

Row 3: knit, increasing 1 st at beg and end of row [10 sts].

Row 4: purl.

Row 5: knit, increasing 1 st at beg and end of row [12 sts].

Rows 6–10: continue in st st.

Row 11: knit, decreasing 1 st at beg and end of row [10 sts].

Row 12: purl.

Row 13: knit, decreasing 1 st at beg and end of row [8 sts].

Row 14: purl.

Cast off.

Making up

Make small ridges going widthways across the side of the cake, holding them in place with rows of running stitches. Stitch the short edges of the cake side together to form a tube. Sew the cake base to one end. Fill with stuffing. Sew the iced top in place. Using the fluffy polyester yarn, make a row of running stitches around the edge of the icing. Decorate the top with multi-coloured yarn and beads. Tie a ribbon around the cake and make a small bow at the front.

The fun pink and green jazzy cake has a green cherry on the top, which is knitted using the holly berry pattern on page 22.

Baby Cup Cake

Materials:

2 balls 4 ply – 1 pink and 1 cream

1 ball 100% cotton 4 ply – white

Pink seed beads

Cardboard for base, 45mm (1¾in) diameter

Stiff, white paper

Toy stuffing

Needles:

1 pair 2.25mm (UK 13; US 1) knitting needles

Set of 4 x 3.25mm (UK 10; US 3) knitting
    needles with points at both ends

Instructions:

Top of cake

Cast on 42 sts using cream wool and double-
ended needles – 14 sts on each of 3 needles.
Rounds 1–5: knit.
Round 6: change to pink and work a K row.
Round 7: (K5, K2tog, K5, K2tog) on each needle
[12 sts on each needle].
Round 8: knit.
Round 9: (K4, K2tog, K4, K2tog) on each needle
[10 sts on each needle].
Round 10: knit.
Round 11: (K3, K2tog, K3, K2tog) on each
needle [8 sts on each needle].
Round 12: knit.
Round 13: (K2, K2tog, K2, K2tog) on each
needle [6 sts on each needle].
Round 14: knit.
Round 15: (K1, K2tog, K1, K2tog) on each
needle [4 sts on each needle].
Round 16: knit.
Round 17: (K2tog, K2tog) on each needle [2 sts
on each needle].
Break yarn, leaving a long end. Thread through
stitches on needles and draw up tightly.

Side of case

Cast on 60 sts using white cotton 4 ply and
2.25mm needles.
Rows 1–11: K1, P1 across each row.
Row 12: inc every second P st across row.
Cast off.

Base of case

Cast on 10 sts using white cotton 4 ply and
2.25mm needles. Work in st st.
Row 1: ** purl.
Row 2: inc 1 st at beg and end of row. **
Rows 3–8: repeat from ** to ** 3 times [18 sts].
Rows 9–11: continue in st st.
Rows 12–18: dec 1 st at beg and end of every K
row [10 sts].
Row 19: purl.
Cast off.

Making up

Join the sides of the cup cake case, then stitch
the bottom in place. Pull up the thread holding
the stitches at the top of the cake, and darn the
thread in to hold it firmly in place. Using stiff
paper, cut a strip large enough to wrap around
the inside of the case. Tape the sides together
to make a paper liner that fits inside the case
– this will make the case stiffer and stop it losing
its shape. Tape the cardboard base to the
paper liner, insert into the knitted case, then
fill the case and the top of the cake with toy
stuffing. Put the top on the case and sew them
together at the edges. Sew seed beads to the
top of the cup cake.

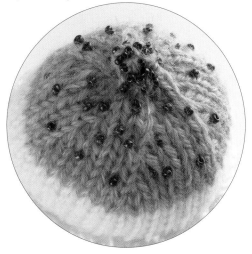

*The pretty baby-blue cup cake is made using blue
and white 4 ply wool. Blue seed beads and a teddy
button have been sewn to the top.*

Swiss Roll

Materials:

2 balls cotton double knitting yarn – 1 beige and 1 raspberry

Needles:

1 pair 3.25mm (UK 10; US 3) knitting needles

Instructions:

Outer layer

Using beige cotton, cast on 20 sts.
Rows 1–60: st st.
Cast off.

Inner layer

Using raspberry cotton, cast on 20 sts.
Rows 1–50: st st.
Cast off.

Making up

With the smaller rectangle on top and the two short edges together, roll up the two layers tightly and evenly to form a Swiss roll. Turn under the end of the outer knitted layer and stitch in place.

The chocolate Swiss roll is made using chocolate and cream double knitting wool.

Christmas Holly Cake

Materials:

1 ball double knitting – white

Small amount of green and red double knitting

18mm (¾in) Christmas ribbon, 25cm (9¾in)

Toy stuffing

Needles:

1 pair 2.5mm (UK 12; US 2) knitting needles

1 pair 3.25mm (UK 10, US 3) knitting needles

Set of 4 x 2.5mm (UK 12; US 2) knitting needles with points at both ends

Instructions:

Top of cake

Cast on 51 sts using white wool and double-ended needles – 17 sts on each of 3 needles.

Rounds 1–26: knit.

Round 27: * dec 2 sts randomly on each needle * [15 sts on each needle].

Rounds 28–33: repeat from * to * [3 sts on each needle].

Round 34: K2tog, K1 [2 sts on each needle].

Break yarn, leaving a long end. Thread through stitches on needles and draw up tightly.

Base of cake

Cast on 12 sts using white wool and 2.5mm needles and work in st st.

Row 1: ** purl.

Row 2: knit, increasing 1 st at beg and end of row. **

Rows 3–8: repeat from ** to ** [20 sts].

Rows 9–11: continue in st st.

Rows 12–18: dec 1 st at beg and end of every K row [12 sts].

Row 19: purl.

Cast off.

Holly

Make two leaves.

Cast on 2 sts using green wool and 3.25mm needles.

Rows 1–2: work in st st, starting with a K row.

Row 3: inc both sts [4 sts].

Rows 4–6: st st.

Row 7: inc first and last st [6 sts].

Row 8: purl.

Row 9: inc first and last st [8 sts].

Row 10: purl.

Row 11: K2tog at beg and end of row [6 sts].

Row 12: purl.

Row 13: repeat row 11 [4 sts].

Row 14: purl.

Row 15: K2tog, K2tog.

Row 16: P2tog.

Berries

Make three berries.

Cast on 5 sts using red wool and 3.25mm needles.

Rows 1–5: st st.

Cast off.

Making up

Pull up the thread at the top of the cake holding the remaining stitches, then darn the thread end into the stitches at the back of the knitting. Stuff the domed cake with toy stuffing then stitch it on to the cake base. Wrap a length of ribbon around the cake, overlapping the ends before stitching it in place. Make a row of gathering stitching around the edge of the knitted berry. Add a small amount of toy stuffing to the centre, then pull up the thread and secure. Stitch the holly leaves and the berries to the top of the cake.

The holly and berries have been replaced by a charming Christmas rose on this alternative version of the domed Christmas holly cake. The rose is knitted using the flower pattern on page 38. Follow the instructions until row 7 [64 sts], then cast off in purl. Small holly-shaped beads have been used to decorate the cake.

Muffin

Materials:

1 ball bobbly nylon double knitting – pink
1 ball fluffy polyester yarn – cream
Toy stuffing
Heart-shaped button

Needles:

1 pair 3.25mm (UK 10; US 3) knitting needles

Instructions:

Cast on 35 sts in pink. Work in g st.
Rows 1–17: inc 1 st at beg and end of row 2, and then beg and end of every third row [47 sts].
Row 18: break yarn and change to fluffy yarn. K to end of row.
Row 19: break yarn and change back to pink. Inc every third st across row [62 sts].
Rows 20–23: change to st st, starting with a K row.
Row 24: * knit every fifth and sixth sts together across row * [52 sts].
Rows 25–27: st st.
Row 28: repeat from * to * [44 sts].
Row 29: purl.
Row 30: repeat from * to * [37 sts].
Rows 31–32: change to fluffy yarn and work in g st.
Row 33: repeat from * to * [31 sts].
Row 34: repeat from * to * [26 sts].
Row 35: knit.
Break yarn, leaving a long end. Thread through stitches on needle, draw up tightly and fasten off.

Making up

With wrong sides facing, sew up the side seam of the muffin. Turn right-side out. Stuff the bottom half of the muffin lightly – do not put stuffing in the top or you will not achieve a good muffin shape. Gather up the bottom, and secure the thread. Make rows of running stitches around the top edge of the muffin base, just under the row of fluffy yarn, and pull up lightly – this will help to shape the bottom of the muffin. Pull the top into shape over the base and stitch a heart-shaped button to the top.

The chocolate muffin has been knitted in dark brown yarn to create a cake that really does look good enough to eat. The cherry is knitted in red yarn and covered in red seed beads using the berry instructions on page 14.

Lemon Meringue

Materials:

2 balls double knitting – 1 beige and 1 yellow

1 chunky snowflake yarn – white

Cardboard for insert, 9 x 12cm (3½ x 4¾in)

Toy stuffing

Brown felt-tipped pen

Needles:

1 pair 3.25mm (UK 10; US 3) knitting needles

Instructions:

Base and back of pastry case

Cast on 14 sts in beige.

Rows 1–6: work in st st, starting with a K row.

Row 7: purl across a K row.

Rows 8–12: work in st st, starting with a P row.

Row 13: K1, K2tog, K to last 3 sts, K2tog, K1 [12 sts].

Rows 14–16: work in st st, starting with a P row.

Row 17: K1, K2tog, K to last 3 sts, K2tog, K1 [10 sts].

Rows 18–20: work in st st, starting with a P row.

Row 21: K1, K2tog, K to last 3 sts, K2tog, K1 [8 sts].

Rows 22–24: work in st st, starting with a P row.

Row 25: K1, K2tog, K to last 3 sts, K2tog, K1 [6 sts].

Rows 26–28: work in st st, starting with a P row.

Row 29: K1, K2tog, K2tog, K1.

Row 30: purl.

Row 31: K2tog, K2tog.

Row 32: purl.

Row 33: K2tog.

Break yarn, leaving a long end. Thread through last stitch on needle.

Sides of pastry case and filling

Pick up and knit 25 sts in beige along one edge of the triangular pastry case base.

Row 2: purl.

Rows 3–7: change to yellow and work in st st for 5 rows.

Cast off on a P row. Repeat for the other side of the pastry case.

Pastry crust

The crust along the top edge of the back of the slice is made using the instructions for piped cream on page 6. Using beige wool, make a row of 3 swirls.

Meringue topping

Pick up and knit 14 sts in white along the top edge of the back of the slice.

Rows 2–4: work in st st, starting with a P row.

Row 5: * K1, K2tog, K to last 3 sts, K2tog, K1 * [12 sts].

Rows 6–8: work in st st, starting with a P row.

Row 9: repeat from * to * [10 sts].

Rows 10–12: work in st st, starting with a P row.

Row 13: repeat from * to * [8 sts].

Rows 14–16: work in st st, starting with a P row.

Row 17: repeat from * to * [6 sts].

Rows 18–20: work in st st, starting with a P row.

Row 21: K1, K2tog, K2tog, K1 [4 sts].

Row 22: purl.

Row 23: K2tog, K2tog [2 sts].

Row 24: K2tog.

Break yarn, leaving a long end. Thread through last stitch on needle.

Try knitting the chocolate version of the meringue slice – just replace the lemon wool with chocolate.

Making up

On the wrong side of the knitting, stitch the sides of the pastry case to the back, and stitch the front edges together to form a point. Fold a strip of cardboard into a triangular shape to line the sides and back of the slice. It is important to make the cardboard shape slightly larger than the knitting, so that the knitting can be stretched over it. This will give a neater finish. Insert the cardboard into the slice, and fill with toy stuffing. Stretch the meringue over the top of the slice and stitch it to the filling. Sew the pastry crust to the back of the slice. Use a brown felt-tipped pen to colour the meringue to give it a cooked appearance.

Carrot Cake

Materials:

2 balls double knitting – 1 flecked cream and
   1 beige

1 ball bobbly nylon double knitting – off-white

Small amount of double knitting in orange
   and green

Brown, walnut, peach and cream seed beads

Cardboard for insert, 8 x 25cm (3¼ x 9¾in)

Toy stuffing

Needles:

1 pair 3.25mm (UK 10; US 3) knitting needles

Instructions:

Follow the instructions for the Chocolate
Gateau on page 6. The top of the cake is
knitted in bobbly double knitting, the back and
base in flecked double knitting with the centre
layer in beige. Knit two rows of 3 piped cream
swirls for the back of the cake in off-white
bobbly wool.

Carrot

Cast on 10 sts in orange.
Row 1: knit.
Row 2: purl.
Row 3: (K1, K2tog) 3 times, K1 [7 sts].
Row 4: purl.
Row 5: (K1, K2tog) twice, K1 [5 sts].
Row 6: purl.
Row 7: knit.
Row 8: purl.
Row 9: K1, K2tog, K1.
Row 10: P3tog.
Break yarn and thread through last stitch on
the needle.

Carrot top

Cast on 2 sts using green wool.
Rows 1–2: g st.
Cast off.

Making up

The carrot cake is assembled in the same way
as the Chocolate Gateau on page 6. Stitch the
two lengths of piped cream swirls to the cake.
Decorate the cake by randomly stitching seed
beads to the back. Stitch the carrot top to the
carrot, and then sew it to the top of the cake.

Viennese Whirl

Materials:

1 ball 4 ply – cream
1 ball fluffy mohair acrylic mix – cream
Small amount of red double knitting
Toy stuffing
Brown felt-tipped pen

Needles:

1 pair 3.25mm (UK 10; US 3) knitting needles
Set of 4 x 2.5mm (UK 12; US 2) knitting needles
with points at both ends

Instructions:

Whirl

For each cake, make four circular whirls.

Cast on 60 sts using cream wool and double-ended needles – 20 sts on each of 3 needles.
Rounds 1–3: knit.
Round 4: knit, decreasing first and last st on each needle [18 sts on each needle].
Round 5: purl, decreasing first and last st on each needle [16 sts on each needle].
Round 6: repeat round 5 [14 sts on each needle].
Round 7: repeat round 4 [12 sts on each needle].
Round 8: repeat round 4 [10 sts on each needle].

Round 9: repeat round 5 [8 sts on each needle].
Round 10: repeat round 5 [6 sts on each needle].
Round 11: repeat round 4 [4 sts on each needle].
Round 12: K2tog, K2tog on each needle [2 sts on each needle].
Round 13: K2tog on each needle [1 st on each needle].
Break yarn, leaving a long end. Thread through stitches on needle and draw up tightly.

Cream

Cast on 10 sts in fluffy mohair acrylic using 3.25mm needles and work in g st.
Row 1: knit.
Row 2: inc 1 st at beg and end of row [12 sts].
Row 3: knit.
Row 4: inc 1 st at beg and end of row [14 sts].
Rows 5–16: st st, starting with a K row.
Row 17: K2tog at beg and end of row [12 sts].
Row 18: knit.
Row 19: K2tog at beg and end of row [10 sts].
Row 20: knit.
Cast off.

Cherry

Cast on 5 sts in red wool using 3.25mm needles.
Rows 1–4: st st.
Cast off.

Making up

Pull up the thread holding the stitches at the top of the whirl, and darn the thread end into the stitches to hold them firmly in place. With wrong sides together, place two whirls together, lightly stuff, then over-stitch the edges. Repeat with the other two whirls. Make a row of running stitches around the edge of the cream then pull up the thread to gather it slightly. Sew the two completed halves of the Viennese whirl together with the cream layer between them. Make a row of gathering stitching around the edge of the knitted cherry. Add a small amount of toy stuffing to the centre, then pull up the thread and secure. Sew the cherry on to the centre top. Use a brown felt-tipped pen to add a few flecks of colour to the edges and top of the whirl.

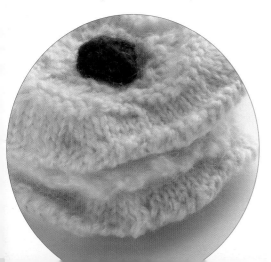

Raspberry Heart Cake

Materials:

2 balls double knitting – 1 flecked pink and
  1 maroon

Small amount of fluffy polyester yarn – cream

Pink ribbon rose

Toy stuffing

Needles:

1 pair 3.25mm (UK 10; US 3) knitting needles

Stitch holder

Instructions:

Top and base of heart

Knit one heart in flecked pink double knitting
and one in maroon double knitting.

Cast on 2 sts.
Rows 1–2: st st, starting with a K row.
Row 3: knit, increasing 1 st at beg and end of
row [4 sts].
Row 4: purl.
Row 5: repeat row 3 [6 sts].
Row 6: purl.
Row 7: repeat row 3 [8 sts].
Row 8: purl.
Row 9: repeat row 3 [10 sts].
Row 10: purl.
Row 11: repeat row 3 [12 sts].
Rows 12–14: continue in st st.
Row 15: knit, increasing 1 st at beg and end of
row [14 sts].
Rows 16–18: continue in st st.
Row 19: repeat row 15 [16 sts].
Row 20: P first 8 sts. Turn and continue working
on these 8 sts. Transfer other sts to stitch holder.
Row 21: * K2tog, K4, K2tog.
Row 22: purl.
Row 23: K2tog, K2, K2tog.
Row 24: purl.
Row 25: K2tog, K2tog.
Row 26: P2tog.

Break yarn, leaving a long end. Thread through
last stitch on needle. *
Transfer 8 sts on stitch holder to needle and
repeat from * to * .

Side of heart

Cast on 10 sts.
Rows 1–75: st st.
Cast off.

Making up

With wrong sides facing, sew the short edges
of the side strip together. Stitch the heart-
shaped top to the side, easing it gently into
shape. Repeat for the base, leaving a small
gap for stuffing. Turn right-side out and fill with
toy stuffing. Stitch up the gap. Stitch a circle of
white fluffy yarn to the top of the heart with the
ribbon rose in the centre.

*The side and base of the alternative version of this
cake have been knitted using pink double knitting
wool. The raspberries are made using the pattern
on page 14.*

Cherry Pie Slice

Materials:

2 balls wool-cotton double knitting – 1 cream and 1 raspberry

Cherry red chunky beads

Cherry red seed beads

Cardboard for base, 7 x 10cm (2¾ x 4in)

Toy stuffing

Needles:

1 pair 3.25mm (UK 10; US 3) knitting needles

Instructions:

Cherry filling

Cast on 18 sts.

Row 1: (right side) purl.

Row 2: K1, * (K1, P1, K1) into next st, P3tog. * Repeat from * to * to last st, K1.

Row 3: purl.

Row 4: K1, ** P3tog, (K1, P1, K1) into next st. ** Repeat from ** to ** to last st, K1.

Row 5: purl.

Row 6: repeat row 2.

Row 7: purl.

Row 8: K1, repeat from ** to ** 3 times, P3tog, K2 [16 sts].

Row 9: purl.

Row 10: K1, repeat from * to * 3 times, (K1, P1, K1) into next st, K2tog [17 sts].

Row 11: P2tog, P to last 4 sts, P2tog, P2tog [14 sts].

Row 12: K2, repeat from * to * 3 times.

Row 13: purl.

Row 14: K1, repeat from * to * 3 times, K1.

Row 15: P2tog, P to last 2 sts, P2tog [12 sts].

Row 16: Repeat from ** to ** twice, P3tog, K1 [10 sts].

Row 17: purl.

Row 18: K1, repeat from ** to ** twice, K1.

Row 19: purl.

Row 20: K1, repeat from * to * twice, K1.

Row 21: purl.

Row 22: K1, repeat from * to * twice, K1 [10 sts].

Row 23: purl.

Row 24: P4tog, repeat from * to * once, (K1, P1, K1) into next st, K1 [9 sts].

Row 25: purl.

Row 26: P4tog, repeat from * to * once, K1 [6 sts].

Row 27: P3tog, P3tog.

Row 28: P2tog.

Cast off.

Base and back of pastry case

Cast on 14 sts in cream.

Rows 1–6: st st, starting with a K row.

Row 7: purl across a K row.

Rows 8–12: work in st st, starting with a P row.

Row 13: K1, K2tog, K to last 3 sts, K2tog, K1 [12 sts].

Rows 14–16: work in st st, starting with a P row.

Row 17: K1, K2tog, K to last 3 sts, K2tog, K1 [10 sts].

Rows 18–20: work in st st, starting with a P row.

Row 21: K1, K2tog, K to last 3 sts, K2tog, K1 [8 sts].

Rows 22–24: work in st st, starting with a P row.

Row 25: K1, K2tog, K to last 3 sts, K2tog, K1 [6 sts].

Rows 26–28: work in st st, starting with a P row.

Row 29: K1, K2tog, K2tog, K1.

Row 30: purl.

Row 31: K2tog, K2tog.

Row 32: purl.

Row 33: K2tog.

Break yarn, leaving a long end. Thread through last stitch on needle.

Sides of pastry case

With right sides facing, pick up and knit 22 sts from one long side of the triangular base.
Rows 1–6: work in st st, starting with a P row.
Cast off.
Repeat for the other side.

Pastry crust

The crust along the top edge of the back of the slice is made using the instructions for piped cream on page 6. Using cream wool, make a row of 4 swirls.

Cream blob

Cast on 8 sts and work in g st.
Row 1: * knit.
Row 2: knit, increasing 1 st at beg and end of row * [10 sts].
Rows 3–8: repeat from * to * until 16 sts remain.
Rows 9–11: knit.
Row 12: ** dec 1 st at beg and end of row [14 sts].
Row 13: knit. **
Rows 14–17: repeat from ** to ** twice [10 sts].
Row 18: repeat row 12 [8 sts].
Cast off.

Making up

With wrong sides facing, sew up the front and back seams of the tart case. Cut a cardboard triangle to fit inside the case. Place it in the bottom and stuff with toy stuffing. Place the knitted cherry filling over the stuffing and stitch to the case. Stitch the pastry crust to the back of the case. To make the cream blob, fold the knitted shape in half lengthways and stitch along the edge. Re-shape the knitting so that the seam runs down the centre, then roll it up and secure with a few stitches. Attach the cream to the cherry filling. Sew beads to the top of the pie.

Plum is the flavour of this alternative pie slice, with the filling stitched using mauve wool-cotton mix. Bugle beads and a blob of cream complete this dessert.

Crazy Cup Cake

Materials:

1 ball big pin knitting yarn – red
1 ball metallic knitting yarn – gold
Cardboard for base, 45mm (1¾in) diameter
Stiff, white paper, 4 x 13cm (1½ x 5in)
Toy stuffing

Needles:

1 pair 4mm (UK 8; US 6) knitting needles
1 pair 3.25mm (UK 10; US 3) knitting needles

Instructions:

Top of cup cake

Using 4mm needles and big pin knitting yarn, cast on 25 sts. Work in g st.
Rows 1–9: knit.
Row 10: * K4, K2tog. * Repeat from * to * to last st, K1 [21 sts].
Row 11: knit.
Row 12: ** K3, K2tog. ** Repeat from ** to ** to last st, K1 [17 sts].
Row 13: knit.
Break yarn, leaving a long end. Thread through stitches on needle and draw up tightly.

Cup cake case

Using metallic thread and 3.25mm needles, cast on 48 sts. Work in rib.
Rows 1–11: (K1, P1) to end.
Row 12: (K1, P1) to end, increasing every second P st.
Cast off.

Case base

Using metallic thread and 3.25mm needles, cast on 8 sts.
Row 1: purl.
Row 2: knit, increasing at beg and end of row [10 sts].
Rows 3–6: repeat rows 1 and 2 twice [14 sts].
Row 7: purl.
Row 8: knit.
Row 9: purl.
Row 10: knit, decreasing at beg and end of row [12 sts].
Row 11–14: repeat rows 9 and 10 twice [8 sts].
Cast off.

Making up

With wrong sides facing, sew up the side seam of the cup cake top. Turn right-side out. Pull up the thread holding the stitches at the top of the cake, and darn the thread end in to hold it firmly in place. With wrong sides facing, sew up the side seam of the cup cake case. Turn right-side out. Stitch the base to the side of the cake. Using stiff paper, cut a strip large enough to wrap around the inside of the case. Tape the sides together to make a paper liner that will fit inside the case – this will make the case stiffer and stop it losing its shape. Tape the cardboard base to the paper liner, insert it in the knitted case, then fill the case and the top of the cake with toy stuffing. Stitch the top to the bottom at the edges.

The blue version of the Crazy Cup Cake is simple to knit in just a couple of hours. The top is knitted using blue big pin knitting yarn and the case is in silver metallic thread.

Angel Cake

Materials:

2 balls 4 ply – 1 pink and 1 pale pink

Short lengths of green wool for leaves

Cardboard for insert, 6 x 20cm (2¼ x 7¾in)

Toy stuffing

Needles:

1 pair 3.25mm (UK 10; US 3) knitting needles

Instructions:

Sides of cake

Cast on 60 sts in pink wool. Work in g st.

Rows 1–5: knit.

Rows 6–7: change to pale pink and work in st st, starting with a K row.

Rows 8–9: change back to pink and continue in st st.

Rows 10–11: change to pale pink and continue in st st.

Rows 12–13: change to pink and continue in st st.

Rows 14–15: change to pale pink and continue in st st.

Rows 16–21: change to pink and work in g st. Cast off.

Top and bottom of cake

Cast on 14 sts.

Rows 1–21: st st.

Cast off.

Flower

Cast on 8 sts using pink. Work in st st.

Row 1: knit.

Row 2: purl.

Row 3: knit, increasing every st [16 sts].

Row 4: purl.

Row 5: knit, increasing every st [32 sts].

Row 6: purl.

Row 7: knit, increasing every st [64 sts].

Row 8: purl.

Row 9: knit, increasing every fourth st across row [80 sts].

Cast off.

Leaves

Cast on 2 sts and work in g st.

Row 1: knit.

Row 2: inc every st [4 sts].

Rows 3–4: knit.

Row 5: inc first and last st [6 sts].

Rows 6–7: knit.

Row 8: K2tog at beg and end of row [4 sts].

Rows 9–10: knit.

Row 11: K2tog, K2tog [2 sts].

Row 12: K2tog.

Break yarn and pull through last stitch.

Making up

Join together the two short edges of the cake side to make a tube. Working on the right side of the knitting, use small running stitches to attach the cake base to the side – working on the right side will make a ridge on the edge of the cake. Roll the cardboard into a flattened tube shape, overlapping the ends, insert it into the cake and stuff. Sew the top on the cake in the same way as the base. Roll the flower up into a pleasing shape and secure it with a few stitches. Attach the flower and the leaves to the top of the cake.

This delicious chocolate version of the angel cake is made using dark brown and cream 4 ply wool.

Wedding Cake

Materials:

4 balls double knitting – 1 white, 1 peach,
  1 dark brown and 1 brown

1 ball cotton double knitting – orange

Gold embroidery thread

Pearl beads

Cardboard for lining, 8 x 30cm (3¼ x 11¾in)

Toy stuffing

Needles:

1 pair 3.25mm (UK 10; US 3) knitting needles

Instructions:

The back, top and base of the cake are knitted
in one piece using white double knitting and
3.25mm needles. The instructions are the same
as for the Chocolate Gateau on page 6.

Sides of cake

Fold the knitted back, top and base so that you
can see which of the two triangular sections will
be the top of your cake. You will be knitting the
side of the cake from the iced top down.

Row 1: with right side facing, pick up and knit
24 sts in white along one side of the
triangular top.
Row 2: purl.
Row 3: change to orange and K to end of row.
Row 4: purl.
Row 5: knit.
Rows 6–24: work in st st using two shades of
brown, starting with a P row. Change colour
randomly across each row to get a mottled fruit
cake effect. Take care to keep tension even as
wool is taken across back of work.
Cast off.
Repeat for other side of cake.

Marzipan on back of cake

Row 1: with right side facing, pick up and knit
24 sts in white down one side of the cake back.
Row 2: purl.
Row 3: change to orange and K to end of row.
Row 4: purl.
Cast off.
Repeat for the other side.

Peach icing balls

Make six individual balls of peach icing – three
for the iced edging along the top of the cake
and three for the base (not shown).
Cast on 2 sts. Work g st for 5 rows. Cast off.

Royal icing

Using the piped cream instructions on page 6,
make two lengths of 4 icing swirls.

Making up

With wrong sides facing, sew the cake sides
together along the front edge. Turn right-side
out. Cut and fold the strip of cardboard into
a triangular shape to fit inside the cake – the
top and bottom are left unlined. It is important
to make the cardboard shape slightly larger
than the knitting, so that the knitting can be
stretched when sewn into place. Line the cake
and fill it with toy stuffing. Sew the cake sides
to the base of the cake. Repeat for the other
side. Ease the marzipan attached to the back of
the cake just under the cake sides and carefully
stitch it in place. Sew the two Royal icing strips
to the back of the cake – one along the top
and one along the base. Sew the peach icing
balls between the Royal icing swirls. Using gold
embroidery thread, stitch a criss-cross pattern
on the back and top of the cake. Sew pearl
beads at the intersections.

Cup Cake Egg Cosy

Materials:

2 balls pure merino – 1 chocolate and 1 pink

1 ball 100% cotton 4 ply – white

Short lengths of pure merino wool in lime green for the embroidery

Needles:

1 pair 2.75mm (UK 12; US 2) knitting needles

1 pair 2.25mm (UK 13; US 1) knitting needles

Instructions:

Top of cup cake

Cast on 36 sts in brown wool using 2.75mm needles.

Rows 1–6: st st.

Rows 7–18: change to pink and work in g st.

Row 19: knit, decreasing 4 sts randomly across row [32 sts].

Row 20: knit.

Row 21: knit, decreasing 4 sts randomly across row [28 sts].

Row 22: knit.

Row 23: knit, decreasing 4 sts randomly across row [24 sts].

Row 24: knit.

Row 25: knit, decreasing 4 sts randomly across row [20 sts].

Row 26: knit.

Break yarn, leaving a long end. Thread through stitches on needle and draw up tightly.

Side of case

Cast on 60 sts using white cotton 4 ply and 2.25mm needles.

Rows 1–11: (K1, P1) to end of row.

Row 12: inc every second P st across row.

Cast off.

Making up

Join the two sides of the case and the cup cake top. Pull up the thread holding the stitches at the top of the cake, and darn the thread end in to hold it firmly in place. Stitch the case to the cake top. Using lime green wool, work sets of four lazy daisy stitches randomly over the top of the cake. If you enjoy a larger breakfast egg, knit the cosy using larger needles!

Why not make a complete set of these stylish egg cosies to match your own kitchen. This alternative design has been made using blue and cream wool and has dark blue lazy daisy stitches embroidered on.

Fruit Fancy

Materials:

3 balls double knitting – 1 lemon, 1 yellow and 1 white

Small amount of green, mauve and orange wool

Black seed beads

Cardboard for insert, 6 x 44cm (2¼ x 17¼in)

Toy stuffing

Needles:

1 pair 3.25mm (UK 10; US 3) knitting needles

Instructions:

Base and top of cake
Make two diamond shapes, one in yellow and one in lemon, for the base and top of the cake.

Cast on 2 sts in yellow or lemon wool.
Rows 1–2: st st, starting with a K row.
Rows 3–14: inc 1 st at beg of every row until 14 sts remain.
Row 15: knit.
Rows 16–27: dec 1 st at beg of every row until 2 sts remain.
Rows 28–29: st st.
Cast off.

Sides of cake
Cast on 60 sts in lemon.
Rows 1–8: st st.
Rows 9–10: change to white and work 2 rows in st st.
Rows 11–17: change back to lemon and work 7 rows in st st.
Rows 18–19: change to yellow and work 2 rows in st st.
Cast off.

Fruit
The fruit is made using the instructions for the fruit tart on page 14. You will need to make one slice of kiwi, three berries and one slice of orange.

Making up
Sew the short edges of the cake side together. Pin the assembled side to the cake base, and at each point of the diamond make a seam on the cake side, working on the wrong side of the knitting, from top to bottom – this will help the cake keep its diamond shape when stuffed. Sew the side of the cake to the base, lining up the seams and the diamond points. Cut a strip of cardboard the same height as the cake, and long enough to fit round the inside of the cake with a small overlap. Bend the cardboard into a diamond shape and insert it into the cake. Fill with toy stuffing, and then attach the top. Sew the fruit to the top of the cake.

The pretty strawberry version of the fruit fancy is made using cream and pink double knitting wool. Lemon slices, berries and a raspberry have been sewn to the top – see instructions on page 14.